STUDIES IN CONTEMPORARY EUROPE

In the past quarter of a century European society, and Europe's relations with the rest of the world, have been radically transformed.

Some of these changes came in the wake of the Second World War; others – and in particular the division of Europe – followed as a result of the Cold War. In addition, throughout the period, other forces, and especially technological change, have been at work to produce a major recasting of the fabric of European society and Europe's role in the world. Many of these changes, together with their attendant problems, have transcended the political and economic divisions of the continent.

The purpose of this series is to examine some of the major economic, social and political developments of the past twenty-five years in Europe as a whole – both East and West – considering the problems and opportunities facing Europe and its citizens today.

STUDIES IN CONTEMPORARY EUROPE

General Editors: ROY PRYCE *and* CHRISTOPHER THORNE

Published titles

AGRICULTURE	HUGH D. CLOUT
RURAL SOCIETIES	S. H. FRANKLIN
YOUTH AND SOCIETY	F. G. FRIEDMANN
EDUCATION	JOHN VAIZEY

In preparation

EUROPE AND THE THIRD WORLD

SOCIAL STRATIFICATION

THE STRUCTURE OF INDUSTRIES

THE URBAN EXPLOSION

POPULATION MOVEMENTS

ECONOMIC PLANNING

THE MASS MEDIA

CHRISTIAN DEMOCRACY

WOMEN IN SOCIETY

SOCIAL DEMOCRACY

PATTERNS OF CO-OPERATION AND INTEGRATION

THE QUEST FOR ECONOMIC GROWTH

YOUTH
AND SOCIETY

F. G. FRIEDMANN

Director, Amerika-Institut, University of Munich

MACMILLAN

First published 1971 by
THE MACMILLAN PRESS LTD
London and Basingstoke
Associated companies in New York Toronto
Dublin Melbourne Johannesburg and Madras

SBN 0333 13307 2

0051713

Printed in Great Britain by
THE ANCHOR PRESS LTD
Tiptree, Essex

301·431
FRI

92091

CONTENTS

PREFACE

Every author and, as a matter of fact, almost every reader knows that a preface is written after a manuscript has been completed. The writer simply details what he has done, then changes the past tense and projects his accomplishments into the future.

The following pages are no exception to this rule. They simply go one step further and anticipate, in diplomatic humility, the criticisms that an essay of this kind is likely to evoke. For, an essay it is, an attempt – as the word suggests – at understanding the various phases and phenomena of youth's attitudes towards society after the Second World War. To be more precise, I have tried to penetrate into the thinking of each major group and to represent it, as it were, from its own point of view. On the other hand, whatever understanding I might have gained I have tried to express in the mental terms and in the vocabulary of an essayist of liberal convictions. By this I mean that I have attempted to convert phenomena of non-verbal communication into more or less rational discourse, and that I have articulated what young people seemed to be striving at in a way that appeared to me reasonable and desirable. I am so bold as to believe that understanding is not only a non-committal, almost patriarchal way of benevolent observation, but also a pre-eminently pedagogical and diplomatic task : to help the individual or group that one observes to find the means for more effective articulation.

Though I have tried to represent a spectrum of the various movements of youth ranging from the hippies and their primarily aesthetic awareness to the radical students and their enhanced political consciousness, the reader will easily distinguish the parts which are based on direct knowledge from parts which reflect indirect and limited information borrowed from the accounts of others, both oral and written. When the subject of this essay was first suggested to me I felt that it was within my grasp to give a short, comprehensive picture of the whole spectrum of phenomena referring to youth. Today I can simply say that I seriously hope that my sketch is informative and controversial enough to stimulate student friends and scholars in the various European countries into correcting my interpretations, where correction is needed, and to enlarge the factual knowledge about ideas and events which in the present essay is all too limited and unsystematic.

It is customary and proper to thank those who have contributed, in one way or another, to the completion of a manuscript. In the present case this is a difficult task. I am able to thank the German Youth Institute in Munich, a government-supported institution, whose library I was able to use, and the colleagues at the Institute of Sociology at the University of Zagreb whom I was able to visit over an extended weekend. The most interesting, and hopefully most fruitful, insights, however, I gained through my daily contacts with students. These contacts were often not of the kind that would call for polite thanks. I am grateful for them as someone might be grateful for being alive or for having been immersed in the mysterious vicissitudes that seem to be an integral part of human destiny.

A few of my students and my junior colleagues have read the manuscript and given their approval. I hesitate, however, to mention their names since it is only fair that I alone bear the responsibility for the many shortcomings of this attempt.

F. G. FRIEDMANN

Munich,
February 1971

8

1. VARIETIES OF YOUTH

'Youth' may conventionally be defined as the group of human beings who have reached the end of puberty but have not yet acquired the full rights and duties of adult life. Foremost among these rights and duties are marriage and earning a livelihood both for oneself and for one's family. It is clear that the time interval occupied by 'youth' depends on the type of culture and society in which an individual lives as well as on the social standing he enjoys. In so-called primitive societies the interval is close to zero : at the end of puberty, the young man or woman is accepted as an adult into the community. The traditional rites of passage mark the importance of this event. Also, in societies in which child labour or the pre-arranged marriage of children is the rule, 'youth' is limited to members of the classes whose sons and daughters are exempt from such labour and consequently enjoy a certain degree of leisure. In civilisations like the Athens of Pericles or the Florence of the Renaissance the scions of the educated and well-to-do families had a sufficiently long period of time between puberty and the responsibilities of adulthood to prepare themselves for the life that corresponded to their social status.

Only as a consequence of advanced industrialisation has 'youth' become a phenomenon of broader social significance. On the one hand, the greater part of the working classes is able to enjoy an ever larger amount of leisure time; on the other hand, there has been a continuous increase in the time necessary for the professional preparation of those who aspire to middle- or upper-level positions. In all this the Second World War has been a turning-point of great significance. It is true that the first years after the war were spent in most countries of Europe repairing the damage caused by the holocaust or strengthening regimes which had come into power during the overture or the aftermath of the war. Soon, however, young people realised that the values and goals that had been defended in the war had lost their significance or, as they liked to put it, their relevance both as far as the contents of leisure time and the contents and modes of higher education were concerned. In other words, the so-called conflict of the generations understood as the personal tensions between fathers and sons had become relatively unimportant compared to the more general question of the attitude of youth to society.

Practically, in dealing with young people of the working classes we shall occupy ourselves with a younger age group – with youths between the ages of fourteen and twenty or twenty-two – since young workers and apprentices take up the duties of adulthood much earlier than middle-class youth. Their anger or rebellion is, at first, a blind and apolitical one; only as young adults do they take a more rational and systematic attitude, through membership of a party or through the use of economic and political weapons like the strike. In dealing with students, secondary-school pupils and 'drop-outs', we shall consider instead groups of youths whose middle-class standing allows – or forces – them to be 'young' until an age that corresponds roughly to the time of the last academic examinations, in other words often until they are twenty-eight or thirty years old. Their approach to society may then be either aesthetic in the sense of a 'new awareness' or primarily ideological in the ways of an enlarged 'political consciousness'.

GANGS AND MASS COMMOTIONS

Among lower-class adolescents we find two phenomena which are of interest to us: the existence of gangs[2] and the occasional large-scale commotions which are not always caused by gangs but in which gangs may participate. The great majority of gangs are composed of underprivileged young people. They are likely to be unskilled labourers and their families have probably suffered economic hardships.

It appears that the lower-class phenomenon of gangs and the middle-class phenomenon of hippydom are little developed in countries where the family structure is still intact, in particular where the family is closer to the extended rather than to the nuclear type; or where there exists a large oppositional Com-

10

munist Party. Thus, there are relatively few gangs or hippies in Italy, France and Spain.

Of course, gangs are not an invention of our time. Whenever young people feel particularly disadvantaged, they tend to turn to their own peers in order to find substitutes for the satisfactions that society refuses to grant them. An example are the so-called razor gangs of Glasgow which flourished during the economic depression following the First World War. After the Second World War gangs appeared in practically all the industrial nations. In England they were called 'Teddy boys', 'Rockers' and 'Mods', in Germany 'Halbstarke', in France 'blousons noirs', in Sweden 'skinnkutter', in Denmark 'underumper', in Italy 'vitelloni', in Holland 'nozum' and in Poland 'hooligans'.

One of the major reasons for their appearance may be seen in the discrepancy between the economic and social status of the least privileged sectors of working-class youth and the growing affluence of society in general. The adolescent's desire for self-affirmation and for status according to models which were usually suggested by the mass media was stunted by his family background, by his limited schooling, and by the lack of interest on the part of a self-satisfied society.

The timeless problems of the adolescent were heightened in the 1950s by difficulties which arose out of his insecure position in a particular time and society. The weakening of the family and other institutions responsible for certain aspects of the process of socialisation, of church, party or school, enhanced the interest of the young in finding individual identity through active participation in groups of their peers. Self-affirmation usually found expression in either one of two ways: in self-representation through outlandish forms of dress, hair style, posture, gait, or in noisy exuberance in personal ways of aggression. In the first case we have the dandy style of the Teddy boys as a protest against the drabness of adult working-class life. Their gatherings took place in little cafés – which emphasised, in a somewhat pitiful way, the modish character and limitations of their revolt. The second group sought instead every possible occasion to provoke the common citizen by destroying property, by looking for brawls at any price, by noisy motor-cycle races. Their dark leather jackets were meant to underline their manliness in a society which refused to accept the emancipation of adolescents. The motor-cycle fad may be seen as an appropriation of certain aspects of technology in the service of conspicuous manliness. All these phenomena, no doubt, were expressions both of (misdirected) youthful exuberance and of deep frustration.

The lower-class gangs are typically hordes rather than stable groups organised on the basis of an ideology. Even the activities of the more violent type originated on the spur of the moment. This was even true of confrontations between gangs – for example, the notorious battles between the British Mods and Rockers around Whitsun 1964. They were not premeditated but – similar to confrontations with the police – evidently occurred when a latent mood found an often trivial occasion for explosive expression. Even the crimes committed by gangs were mostly of a casual nature. They happened as by-products of some larger commotion or of attempts to obtain as quickly as possible the money necessary for securing the style set, respectively, by their own group or by the mass media which doted on the whims of the young in the interests of the producers of fashionable goods.

Besides the gangs, with their relatively fixed code of behaviour, we see rather volatile masses of young people taking part in large-scale commotions which lasted from a few hours to several days. Sociologists have not yet found an appropriate term[3] for such phenomena. For the participants neither constitute an 'amorphous mass' nor a large-scale organised group. Whatever the specific reason for an event, the psychological basis for violent behaviour seemed to have been a collective desire for revenge for having been slighted on this or on previous occasions because of belonging concurrently to two weak and insecure groups – to youth and to the lower classes. In the suddenly assembled, surging mass the individual thought he could find protection against the adult authorities of the ruling middle-class world. He also felt that he was momentarily immune from any form of personal responsibility. Being surrounded by a surging mass of people with similar feelings, he was free from the powers that under normal circumstances slighted his ego and overwhelmed his person; in fact, he was able to make his own collective power felt in a destructive orgy that included the exhilarating noise of shattered glass, the fascination of the flame and the thrill of the plundering crowd.

12

Most of the large-scale riots occurred in the second half of the fifties. They took place from Stockholm to Zürich and from Paris to Berlin. We know today that they were largely stimulated by the mass media which lionised the unruly young and gave them what they had so far lacked – a great deal of attention. The immediate causes were manifold. During the Nottingham and Notting Hill race riots of 1958 a number of young people from socially weak groups vented their spleen against groups who were disadvantaged to a still greater degree. Their vicious desire to inflict damage was perhaps enhanced by the fact that the inferiority of the adversary reminded them of their own inferiority : they tended to convert a deep-seated self-hate into the hate of others. In the case of the so-called concert riots, young people who could not get tickets or found a police order objectionable smashed everything they could get hold of in order to liberate themselves from accumulated feelings of hurt and frustration. These pent-up feelings were released while the participants identified themselves with a popular musical star who also came from a discriminated world – a black man, a youth, a drug addict – yet 'had made it' in terms of money and prestige in a world that basically disdained him. His 'doing his own thing' with such striking success, yet looking down upon the world by whose rules he had gained his triumph, was perhaps the greatest satisfaction for his followers.

In Germany the first large-scale riot of 'Halbstarke' occurred in 1955 in front of the Hanover railway station. The riots soon spread to Berlin and to other German and Austrian cities until they petered out in 1957. 1955 also saw three days and nights of rioting in the centre of Paris and subsequently on the French Riviera. A typical concert riot occurred in 1959 in Zürich on the occasion of an appearance by Louis Armstrong. In 1962 large-scale rioting took place in Schwabing, the bohemian suburb of Munich.

In contrast with the life of the gangs and the mass commotions of the fifties, the following decade was characterised by other developments. Gangs continued to exist but played a less spectacular role. The part of lower-class youth which was primarily interested in dress and popular music distinguished itself less from middle-class youth than it had done during the fifties.

13

Among middle- or upper-middle-class youths a whole spectrum of movements existed which reached from the hippies at one end to the radical students at the other. Hippies represented a new emphasis on 'awareness' or a primarily aesthetic sensibility; the student radical Left attempted to intensify and enlarge its political 'consciousness'. These two kinds of emphasis corresponded to two basic connotations of the word 'interest' (one derived from the French, the other from medieval Latin): of being attracted by a work of art, by sport or play, and of being preoccupied with one's economic and political fortunes. The hippies' protest was based on withdrawal from the existing society, on 'opting' or 'dropping *out*'; the political protest occurred *within* the existing society and was considered, at least by its extreme adherents, as the beginning of an attempt at overthrowing that order and at setting another one in its place. In between hippies and radical students we find a number of movements such as the Yippies, the provos and the 'kabouters'. But even hippies may be politicised and radical students full of aesthetic interests; or one and the same person may more or less regularly move back and forth from one end of the scale to the other.

The immediate predecessor of the hippies was the 'beat generation'. It originated in the fifties in California under the guidance of writers like Allan Ginsberg and Jack Kerouac. They were 'beat' or overwhelmed by the modern world and tried, through meditation, hiking in the mountains, and restless riding around the country, to find some form of enlightenment. The hippy movement is said to have received its name from a headline which appeared in 1965 in the *San Francisco Examiner*. (That their name was given to them by critics they share with such originally dissident religious movements as the Puritans or the Methodists.)

The hippy part of the youth protest is often called a substitute or an 'underground'. This is only justified if the term is used in a very broad, almost metaphoric way. For what we see is neither a subculture in the sense of being inferior to a majority culture, nor can we speak of a true counter-culture, since the hippy culture does not aggressively and systematically set itself up against the dominant culture. 'Underground', on the other hand, has a number of meanings, from Dostoevsky's existential under-

14

ground man to the anti-Nazi political and military underground organisation, to the underground world of the criminal. 'Alternative culture' (a term which Dieter Baake suggests) seems to give a clearer picture of what hippies and other young people try to attempt. In all this hippies do not act as an organised group, nor do they have an official programme. They are simply individuals or loosely related, shifting groups having certain longings in common which find their expression in a 'life style'. To this style belongs a kind of demeanour and clothing, a longing for happiness in immediate, spontaneous, primarily aesthetic experience, and an interest in non-verbal, non-intellective communication which is expected to lead to new forms of community. It is this non-verbal, non-intellective element which makes it difficult to give a reliable account of the hippies' efforts.

The outward demeanour is marked by a certain lassitude, by a disdain of the discipline that is thought to be characteristic of successful and socially acceptable behaviour in industrially advanced societies. Hair style, which may be variously interpreted as corresponding to a pre-Raphaelite Christ-image or to the romantic conception of the noble savage, is supplemented by fashions in dress that suggest both a certain sloppiness and the dignity and ease of the archaic. It would be wrong to speak here of conscious motives. And yet it does not seem far-fetched to speak of an instinctive aversion towards the 'cold' correctness of a world which produced with perfect efficiency the marvels of technology, including the atomic bomb, as well as the by-products of peaceful industry that increasingly clutter and poison our environment.

On the other hand, its very attempt at being different makes the hippy culture the victim of a most successful commercial exploitation. For, particularly in a rapidly changing world, fashions play on the new and the extravagant. They stimulate and exploit the youthful desire to be up to date, to be ahead of the times together with one's peers. Peer-group conformity is one of the most important motives upon which the commercial interests feed. This does not exclude the consumer industry being significantly affected by the youth culture itself. At any rate, the first large study of youth was undertaken by an institute of market research.

In contrast with the cultural pessimism which permeates the adult world, hippies try to emphasise joy in life, man's right to

15

happiness. Distrusting the conventional efforts connected with most of the achievements of modern life, they seem to believe in the possibility of an almost immediate, effortless return to an original paradise. In this they share the faith of the religious denominations that believe in a sudden conversion and in the independence of such a conversion from the actual state of the physical world. The hippy conversion, it is true, is more an aesthetic than a religious one. More precisely, awareness, an enhanced immediacy and spontaneity in the perception of the world, is set against the abstract and indirect means of cognition that are characteristic of modern science, technology and administration. The hippies also realise that, as in all cultures and civilisations, the means of cognition and those of communication are closely related. Awareness – in the original sense of the word *aisthesis* – corresponds to the non-intellective means of communication, to which we must add the media of sex, music, and drugs.

In summarising the basic elements that distinguish the hippy style of life from adult middle-class conceptions, one thinks first of all of Daniel Bell's remark that 'change in cultural sensibility is the most important phenomenon of our time'.[4] Within the hippy world this sensibility is likely to express itself in forms that are both spontaneous and communitarian. Both aspects defy any reification in results that would last beyond the act of experience or of expression itself. Rituals exist but are only symbols of shared experience. In older civilisations, symbols of shared experience had been validated for the younger generation through tradition, represented by the testimony and the authority of the elders. In today's world, experience itself is said to authenticate reality – the reality of experience which is likely to be a 'happening', an unpremeditated, nearly unstructured event.

A further element is the international quality of the hippy experience and way of life : the tramping around the world – so different from the organised travels of the citizen-consumer – the 'turning on', the 'joining of the global village'. This international character of the movement is, compared with the more intellectual character of Marxist internationalism, primarily a matter of emotion and as such an end in itself. In addition, there are the hippy attempts at creating communes and communities. The participants in such attempts favour the peer group as an analogue to

16

the tribe or the extended family over the nuclear family and over organisations that are primarily based on utilitarian considerations. Finally, the hippies reject the ethos of work characteristic of capitalist societies – Marcuse's 'performance principle' – for which they try to substitute the 'pleasure principle'. The more intellectually inclined may agree with the Marxists that not all labour is degrading but only alienated labour. Practically, they attempt to become independent of the existing social and economic system by reducing their material needs to a minimum, by doing odd jobs or by accepting money from their parents.

Outside the Western democracies the 'alternative culture' has only secondary significance. Under the more liberal systems of government hippies represent a style, in the Communist countries or on the Iberian Peninsula only a fashion. Style implies a perfect coincidence of an inner attitude or philosophy and certain outward manifestations such as the mode of dress or the enjoyment of certain music. Fashion refers to the outward manifestations alone which are adopted mostly for secondary reasons. In the Eastern countries there are certainly elements of rebellion against the drabness of everyday life or against overall regimentation. In a relatively liberal Communist country like Yugoslavia hippies represent at most an alternative to the present way of using one's leisure time; the majority of the young accept the basic principles of the socialist system and do not look for a total 'alternative culture' as many young people in the West do. At the same time it is the liberal cultures of the West that permit youths to work or not to work, a situation which is further favoured by the permissive attitude of liberal parents. In the socialist countries everybody is required by law to work. On the Iberian Peninsula, on the other hand, or under the Greek colonels' regime, no large-scale commercialisation of youth fashions in dress or music is possible; in the mass media there is either complete silence about such phenomena or stern condemnation, so that beat music, for example, has been forced to become a more or less private cult.

In Spain, hippies are forbidden. Foreign hippies, who used to be tolerated, are no longer admitted, or if already in the country, are expelled. Only on the Mediterranean coast and on the islands do the police make certain concessions in the interest of the tourist trade.

The use of drugs, today an integral part of the youth culture, is not entirely new to Western civilisation. Narcotics are said[5] to have been used in the early industrial age in order to prevent the children of the poor from disturbing their working mothers and the adult poor from interfering with the functioning of the system. Other narcotic agents are believed to have been used by some of the great minds of the period. Then as now, drugs were in a sense the link between otherwise entirely diverse social or intellectual groupings: they helped the poor to bear the misery of their material and psychic condition and the intellectual elite the growing senselessness of human existence and to gain stimulation for their creative attempts. Today, the sons and daughters of comfortable suburbanites are no less addicted than are the children of the ghetto or of the lower middle class.

Hallucinogenic agents, however, have not always been a matter of indiscriminate experimentation, born of social or cultural despair. In fact, from around the turn of the century until the 1950s it was primarily scientific curiosity that motivated a number of psychologists and philosophers to run controlled experiments in order to discover the nature and significance of the non-intellective powers of man. William James 'ran experiments with narcotics at the same time as he wrote *The Varieties of Religious Experience*. He came to the conclusion that our normal working consciousness, rational consciousness as we call it, is but one special type of consciousness.'[6] Havelock Ellis used *peyote* in his studies which he reported to the Smithsonian Institution. Aldous Huxley, who attempted to recapture the value of neglected cultural traditions, reported his controlled experiments in *Doors of Perception*.[7] Allan Watts describes his psychedelic experiments in *The Joyous Cosmology: Adventures in the Chemistry of Consciousness*.[8]

The first popular report of psychedelic experiences appeared in America in *Life* magazine on 13 May 1957. Its author was a vice-president of the J. P. Morgan banking firm, who, with his wife, had gone to Mexico and had eaten from the 'magic mushroom' which, in turn, had brought forth visionary experiences. The final popularisation of hallucinogenic agents and the beginning of indiscriminate experimentation on the part of the hippy movement was probably caused by Timothy Leary. In 1960 he too went to Mexico where he consumed mescalin. In 1962 he founded the so-called 'International Federation for Inner Freedom'.

Those who defend the use of hallucinogenic agents see in it a means of intensifying awareness. They pit this primarily aesthetic awareness against the predominantly intellectual and functional character of our civilisation. Drugs, they believe, are capable of relieving us from the pressure of an abstract, a-human reality and of setting free our creative forces.

Critics point to the problem of addiction. They suggest that drugs tend to lead young people away from responsible participation in the adult world which they claim to desire. Critics are sceptical of the claim that drugs are able to enlarge our awareness and to make us have contacts with new dimensions of reality. What can be achieved is, at most, that a single ray of light, a single beat overwhelms the individual in a way that excludes all other elements present in normal perception. In other words, he who uses drugs actually falls victim to a reduction of awareness, to a freezing of sensibility, to a fixation, which turns a supposedly liberating means into an enslaving end.

Defenders and critics of the use of drugs would probably agree that drugs enhance *aisthesis*, that is, passive perception; they do not enlarge experience which implies mental activity, a reaching out towards a potential world on the part of an ordering mind. Those who defend the use of drugs add that it is the exclusion of the ordering, controlling mind which allows the individual to give himself entirely to the free play of associations and emotions. They grant that drugs may isolate the user from the external world but believe that it is only the isolation that allows penetration of a different, of an inner world. As to addiction, they see its causes in the disposition and in the emotions of the individual user rather than in the use of drugs itself. He who takes drugs as a last resort in the flight from reality with which he is unable to cope, will later wake up and find the world more terrible than ever. He will soon be on another 'trip'.

Music plays an extremely important role among young people today, independently of their economic standing or aesthetic sophistication. There is the record-player which already for the Teddy boys fulfilled the role of an important status symbol. For lower-class youth the juke-box with its background beat is the source of some kind of stupor in which the café-bar gang finds itself in between rumbles. The beat-cellar on the other hand is the locale for private or semi-private parties of middle-class youth. Pop-concerts gather thousands of music addicts into a hall, while the big rock festivals call hundreds of thousands of young people together under the open sky.

Historically, beat seems to have originated at a time when jazz had reached a point of structural complexity and sophistication that made it inaccessible to the masses. Beat is intentionally more popular and therefore structurally more simple. It goes back to older Negro music and emphasises a heavy beat which activates the psychomotor system of the listener. The volume of the sound has, next to the beat, a decisive function. To 'led it bleed', to turn on whole batteries of loudspeakers (at great rock festivals over a thousand are in use), together with smell, lights, even sensations of heat or cold – all enhanced by the use of drugs – is said to enable the masses to have experiences of mystic ecstasy. At such moments the individual participant does not melt away into the mass, disappear as an individual, but finds his self confirmed by the analogy between his own experience and the experience of those surrounding him.

There are, of course, great varieties in the field of beat, and of popular music in general. On one hand we find a normal text combined with a normal beat, a text which might be politically tinged; on the other hand we encounter the phenomenon of almost hypnotised masses with hard, hectic responses to a singer's verbal and musical provocation which are apt to remind us of similar hectic and hypnotised responses of the fanatical masses at the Nuremberg Nazi Party rallies. One thing appears to be certain : music – more perhaps even than drugs or the new awareness of youth in general – constitutes today the dividing line between young and old (across which communication does not seem possible). This stands in contrast to the folk songs before the First World War and the artificially cultivated songs of the youth movements between the wars which united people irrespective of age.

Perhaps the first high point of the hippy movement in Europe took place in June 1965 when about 7000 young people gathered in London's Royal Albert Hall to hear beatnik poets recite from their works. That it was even then something of an individualised revival meeting seems to be documented by the film *Wholly Communion*, which was produced during the meeting. In July 1969, 200,000 young people attended at Hyde Park in London a memorial concert for Brian Jones of the Rolling Stones. 300,000 met in August 1969 on the Isle of Wight.

YIPPIES, PROVOS AND 'KABOUTERS'

The Yippies (an abbreviation for Youth International Party) go an important step beyond the hippy protest. Their protest, too, uses primarily aesthetic means, but they are applied to provoke the existing society into revealing itself as working, behind the pretence of humaneness and democracy, *against* the freedom and dignity of the individual. Aesthetic awareness as metapolitics, or the political uses of aesthetics, are, of course, not inventions of today's youth. Rhetoric as an aesthetic device in the service of politics has existed since ancient times. In more recent years it was particularly the theatre that opened itself to experimentation with the avowed purpose of provoking the audience towards keener political awareness. One may think of Brecht's use of the *Verfremdungseffekt*, of the documentary theatre, of the 'Living Theatre' – all attempts at using the legitimate stage for new purposes and, by doing so, closing the gap that traditionally existed between audience and performers.

A forerunner of the youth protest of the sixties and a link between the critical use of the legitimate stage and the street theatre of the radical students was John Osborne, a leading exponent of the 'Angry Young Men' and their dissatisfaction with the British welfare state. *Look Back in Anger*, which at its première in 1956 caused a scandal, was an expression of the revolt of the young individual against the stagnant, commercialised, snobbery-ridden, capitalist middle-class environment. Osborne showed young people in a situation determined by the discrepancy between official ideals and social reality. His play affected young people in many countries who were able to identify themselves with his heroes.

The Yippies use the street, the auditorium of a university, a church for a stage. Theirs is an aggressive sensibility that tears the mask of respectability from the face of institutions. They use uniforms and military equipment in mockery, disturb solemn academic processions by releasing colourful toy balloons, reveal the hypocrisy of Christian sermons by interspersing them with questions about Vietnam, and by obscene interruptions of court proceedings cause judges to make fools of themselves. In all these provocations they move in directions that had been taken by artists as early as the Futurists, Dadaists and Surrealists and further developed by the practitioners of action painting, pop art and simple 'happenings'.[9]

One characteristic of Yippie action is its entirely unstructured nature. In fact, it has been called 'Castroism applied to art: one acts and, through action, discovers the aims of the revolution'.[10] These aims are only a fleeting content of the action, if a content at all. For Yippie action is hostile to any verbal interpretation, any conceptualisation through the intellect. In this it is said to be similar to abstract art which eschews any interpretable content or to pop art which has a content so blatant that it too is beyond any attempts at interpretation. Like Futurists, Dadaists and Surrealists, Yippies carry within themselves the joy of permanent self-destruction. As the Surrealists wanted to go 'beyond art' by the destruction of culture (of what might become structure, permanence), the Yippies are wont to celebrate their own funeral in order to avoid the deadly sins of institutionalisation and ideological fixation.

We should probably add that aggressive sensibility implies not only provocation of an established order but a kind of self-assertion through naked defiance which may result in outbursts of violence. History has shown that the most cruel forms of violence are not too distant relatives of romantic sensibility. Today, the aesthetic sensibility of the Yippies is closely akin to the violence implied in Malcolm X's *Autobiography* or Eldridge Cleaver's *Soul on Ice*, or advocated in Frantz Fanon's *The Wretched of the Earth*. Is there any way of distinguishing between good and bad violence, particularly if we are told that we must not try to find norms that lie outside of the action itself?

The provo and 'kabouter' movements in Holland are two more examples of a primarily aesthetic protest against the shortcomings of the existing society. As with the hippies, the increasing leisure-time at the disposal of the young played an important part in the origin of provos and 'kabouters'. To this one must add that

Holland in recent years has initiated no wars, has not been actively involved with colonial possessions or plagued by race tensions or other forms of social discrimination.[11] These blessings have meant that there has been much youthful energy with few creative outlets in a society governed by middle-class standards of behaviour, including the pressure for ever-greater consumption. The provos – and in this they were closer to the Yippies than to hippydom – tried to operate *within* society. Compared with the Yippies their behaviour was, no doubt, equally provocative though less volatile; they were more political, if political means acting to bring about social and economic change.

The provo movement received its name from its primary purpose – to provoke. In this they take part in the 'new enlightenment'. While the neo-Marxists concentrate primarily on the intellectual tasks of unmasking the contradictions inherent in late-capitalist society, in revealing the ruling consciousness as a 'false consciousness' and the dominant values and ideas as the ideological instruments to cover up the true interests of the ruling classes, the provos try by 'aesthetic' means of provocation to lead to the direct perception of such contradictions. The principal place of provocation was the street, where they distributed pamphlets, campaigned in the nude, performed happenings, threw fire-crackers against the royal coach and battled with the police. As with other groups of young people in practically every modern country, provoking the police had the purpose of forcing an all-pervading, mostly invisible and anonymous authority to show its concrete, tangible face; to penetrate the myth of the well-functioning, well-meaning, non-violent democratic society – the antipode of the unruly, restless, questioning youth – and to show it up as being based not on enlightened interest but on brutal force.

The battles with the forces of public order were accompanied by two phenomena which eventually contributed to the end of the provo movement and, later, to the birth of the 'kabouters'. One phenomenon was the attraction that violent confrontations exercised on other groups, primarily on the 'nozum' gangs which joined the battle and vitiated, in a sense, its original meaning. Another phenomenon was the reaction of the citizens. Most of them were shocked into demanding a vigorous defence of decency rather than into a greater awareness of the contradictions of the social order.

Characteristic of the provos and later of the 'kabouters' was the 'ludike' element, the element of play. Already in 1964 one of the provo leaders had demanded that life should be transformed back into play. Also, where play was used as a means of provocation, as an equivalent to the Socratic irony, it was to be more than the put-on play of the street theatre. As antithesis to the 'game of life' which was played by the conventional rules of society, playfulness was the attitude of the child that is hidden in every man, the Dionysian element, the counterweight to the hypertrophy of the intellect. The need for the play-impulse to find new outlets, as well as the increased possibilities of creating them, was primarily determined by the very nature of our technological society. The cybernetic society allows ever more time for play and playfully creative work. Not only at the beginning of our individual life, when the needs of the child are still taken care of by the parents, is play the central activity, but also in the late stages of scientific and technological development, when our needs are fulfilled by modern production and social security, does play again become a major element. One may think of the mindless 'play' of some of the affluent, the *dolce vita* of those whose antics fill the pages of our illustrated magazines. More interesting is the enjoyment that scientists find as they 'play' with ideas or experiment with hypotheses. Most exciting of all is the 'play' of life, the self-critical, self-ironical game of self-affirmation in an atmosphere that allows spontaneity and experimentation as well as openness to the world and to one's fellow men. This is what provos and 'kabouters', following their compatriot Huizinga, would like to understand as the basis of 'culture'.

Though provos are against any form of rigid or hierarchical organisation, there are informal ways of making decisions and a number of recognised personalities who set the general tone and develop the social programme. This general tone is occasionally anarchistic but not such as to prevent the provos from running candidates in local elections. In fact, in 1966 they succeeded in electing one of their own group to a seat in the Amsterdam city council. They also had a broad civic programme consisting of a number of so-called 'white plans' : white bicycles were to take the place of cars in the inner city; these bicycles stood free of charge at anybody's disposal. (The plan was aborted by the interference of the police.) A second plan referred to 'white chimneys', to chimneys which did not produce any smog. A third plan called for 'white policemen', policemen who were actually social workers.

In world politics the provos were radical pacifists. In their own circles, however, they were unable to agree on whether non-violent means should be supplemented on certain occasions by violent ones. In 1967 a split occurred in the movement on this issue which contributed to its dissolution. In a sense, the 'kabouters' are the heirs to the non-violent section of the provos. They were born in 1970 at a gathering in a student café in Amsterdam. One proposal before the group was to transform the remnants of the provo movement into an army for sabotage with the ultimate goal of taking over the powers of the state. The other, winning, proposal was to turn away from public demonstrations and battles with the police and to work like 'kabouters', like gnomes, for social and political betterment. Roel van Duijn, the leading 'kabouter', speaks of a theory of the two hands': 'with the left hand the kabouters must work on building an alternative society, with the right they must infiltrate the existing society. The new society has no government; it governs itself. It is socialist but this socialism is different from how it was formerly, not any more bureaucratic and centralised. It is decentralised and anti-authoritarian. It is no longer the socialism of the clenched fist, but of the tender hand.'[12]

In the place of provocation the 'kabouters' put in effect certain alternatives to practices of the existing society. This does not exclude an element of humour or mockery. Thus, they created their own 'Orange Free State', an allusion to the Dutch royal house, an *Official Gazette* and various ministries. These, of course, do not emphasise power and dignity but simplicity and everyday social service. The *Official Gazette* publishes a list of the many empty houses in Amsterdam; the 'Ministry of Housing', a small attic room, serves a young theology student who gives advice to citizens looking for housing. A group of 'kabouters', the so-called 'krackers', break into empty houses and ask homeless families to occupy them. Some empty houses are fitted with placards reading 'I am ashamed of myself. Inhabit me!' As a consequence, police

25

and the city administration now seek to mediate between the 'krackers' and the proprietors of empty houses. In addition to housing, 'kabouters' fight against the pollution of cities by automobiles; they sit down in main streets to bring traffic to a standstill. They also help elderly people in coping with bureaucratic requirements.

In the 1970 elections to the city council of Amsterdam the 'kabouters' received 11 per cent of the votes and five seats in the forty-five-seat city council. Some leading 'kabouters' thought this too much power and tried to give one of their seats to the representative of another party. In the meantime there have been disagreements among the 'kabouter' councillors, so that one may wonder how long they will keep their council seats. On the other hand, 'kabouters' find serious disagreements among the individualistic members of a non-party only natural. They are even convinced that, like the provos, the 'kabouters' will only last a limited time. The people, however, who have participated in these movements of heightened awareness and social service will not disappear. And there will be other people and other movements to try to carry on the work for a more individualistic and co-operative world.

The development of the political consciousness of academic youth is more difficult to trace than that of the primarily aesthetic awareness. For in the political realm we must assume, in addition to immediately visible events – to demonstrations, riots, public debates – on the one hand secret deliberations and hidden actions, and on the other hand a lack of political interest and action which has its own political significance. The latter led Schelsky[13] to write of a 'sceptical generation' which he believed dominant in the democratic countries of the West in the decade following the Second World War. Using the terminology of Mannheim,[14] it was not really a 'generation' but a 'generation unit'. A 'generation unit' consists of people who in their own ways interpret and digest the experiences which they have in common with other contemporaries. These experiences included the psychological and ideological let-down after a war which had been fought on both sides with the goal in mind of realising certain ideals, and the necessity of repairing the damage that had been inflicted on one's own country and on one's own security by the events of the war.

A large part of those who were young according to the conventional definition of the term are said to have had an aversion against politics, which they regarded as 'dirty' and dangerous as far as the fulfilment and the protection of their private interests were concerned. They rejected both ideologies and experiments, the two possible approaches towards changing a society. At the same time many of them felt morally and politically safe under the aegis of American democracy, which they experienced both as an assuring routine and, occasionally at least, as an exciting mystique.

In countries like Spain which in the prelude to the Second World War had fallen under a Fascist dictatorship or in Eastern Europe where in the course of the aftermath of the war Communist regimes had taken over, political absenteeism on the part of the young was a far more complex phenomenon. In Yugoslavia, for example, it was the generation of youthful partisans which after the liberation of the country had formed the government and effectuated a revolution of state and society. In Czechoslovakia, after the Communist take-over of 1948, a large part of youth had identified itself with the task of rebuilding a socialist society. Only the betrayal of what they regarded as socialist ideals and the prevention of political participation on the part of the official bureaucracy made them erupt in bitter rebellion. The precise part young people played differed from Budapest to Poznan (both in 1956) and from East Berlin (1953) to Prague (1968). At least in Budapest and Prague they seemed to have been, together with writers and intellectuals, the decisive factor.

2. THE AWAKENING OF POLITICAL
CONSCIOUSNESS

In the liberal democracies of the West it is not yet possible to trace the transition from the so-called sceptical or silent generation to the period of radical political thought and action with any precision. One difficulty lies in the fact that the sociologists who speak of a 'sceptical' or 'silent' generation use primarily quantitative methods which are certainly applicable to a relatively inert and inarticulate group of people, while the political or cultural historians deal with a minority which claims, on the basis of a more highly developed awareness or consciousness, to be a historically significant elite – a term which defies any measurement or precise definition. It is possible, therefore, that the sociologist who trained his eye on the majority within a 'generation' overlooked an elite which, as far as overt actions were concerned, was not yet visible though already in the making. French existentialism – primarily the writings of Sartre and Camus – may, in its individualistic ways, have contributed to the earliest stirrings of the later upheavals.

America, no doubt, played an important part in the awakening of political consciousness in the countries of Western Europe. In this it provided 'both villain and hero'.[15] There were positive and exciting aspects such as the person of President Kennedy. A large number of young people in Europe seemed to have identified themselves with him not because he represented any new philosophy or programme but out of sympathy with his youthful style. This style was eminently aesthetic, which, strange as it may seem, gave his pragmatism a utopian quality. His death plunged the world back into politics as usual. In America, the non-violent techniques of the civil rights movement had appealed to the 'liberal conscience' of the country and stimulated legislation which Congress approved during the first year of the Johnson Administration. The atmosphere in the country, the state of politics, however, had already changed. The young and the black felt increasingly alienated: their demands and expectations found little response on the part of the new political management. The frustrations of the young – and of many who were not so young – finally crystallised around the war in Vietnam and the war in the ghettos.

The preoccupation with Vietnam is said to have contributed to the end of several one-issue campaigns such as the fight by SANE (National Committee for a Sane Nuclear Policy) against atomic armaments or the protest by Easter marchers against war in general. Vietnam, in fact, became the most strident expression of what was wrong with society as a whole, since it was interpreted as a logical outgrowth of the development of the technologically most advanced capitalist country.

At the same time there was an entirely different America that entered and modified the political consciousness of European students. Already in the late fifties and early sixties the American sociological imagination had awakened some European intellectuals to the alarming symptoms of their own advancing mass society. C. Wright Mills, one of the initiators of the American 'New Left', had spoken of the anti-hero of dissent and rejection as agent of social change. Student sit-ins and other forms of non-violent protest had spread all over the South of the United States with considerable success. Finally, confrontations between students and university administrations had broken out, leading to 'teach-ins' and the occupation of university buildings. Police action on a large scale had ensued and led to the débâcle at the 1968 Chicago Democratic Convention and to the killing of students on two campuses. (Even before, young civil rights workers had been slain by racists in the South, while sick minds of a nondescript underground had slain America's most inspiring leaders.)

THE SO-CALLED 'GENERATION CONFLICT'
The student revolt has at times been interpreted as a generational conflict. Upon closer analysis, this judgement applies, at least in the liberal democracies, only in a metaphorical sense. It can be applied almost literally to countries like Yugoslavia or Spain where political movements had come to power by means of a civil or partisan war. The men and women who led these movements soon identified themselves with the state they had taken over and neglected both succeeding events and succeeding generations.

They held on to the achievements of the past, thus losing, under the changing circumstances, their original function and becoming, in an ideological sense, a 'generation'.

In Yugoslavia, the generation of the partisans of the Second World War still holds most of the important political positions. The partisan period, a time of intensive participation, had been followed by a period in which the participation of those who had been too young to be partisans was only formal. This led to dissatisfaction which the ruling party tried to dispel by much talk about the importance of youth. In reality, the official youth organisations tried to integrate young people into the prevailing system and to educate them towards obedience and even subservience. Later, the liberalisation and the anti-Stalinist turn of the party were used by the leaders to cover up the fact that it was still the old generation which ruled.

In Spain, on the other hand, the great majority of the young have no understanding for the generation that fought the Civil War. Nor do they see any reason why they should cling to a system which is the direct outcome of that event.

In Czechoslovakia[16] it was primarily the war generation which was responsible for the socio-political and economic reconstruction in the years 1945–52. This decidedly political generation participated in February 1948 in the Communist take-over of power. A second post-war group was characterised during the years between 1949 and 1955 by a revolutionary enthusiasm, including the hope of changing the world. Though still a part of the first generation, this second group was more romantic than the first since it had no chance to measure its own convictions against those of the adversary; it therefore accepted the doctrine of socialism in a relatively shallow and dogmatic way like a religious creed that is beyond discussion. Its possibilities of taking part in the exercise of power were less than those of the first group. This was due, in part, to the war in Korea and the Cold War, two events which cut the country off not only from the West but also from its own revolutionary past.

The next generation in Czechoslovakia which took the place of part of the first was able to play only a relatively passive role. At the same time, the younger people became imbued with a heightened sense of doubt and insecurity, in contrast to the absolute certainty which was characteristic of the immediate post-war situation. Primary values were now personal happiness, material success, family, and technical knowledge, in addition to regard for individual worth irrespective of political convictions.

Since 1961 or 1962 politics seem to have become more interesting again for young people. Socialism, no doubt, has become for the young as much a matter of fact as has the capitalist system for Western youth. What they realise however, is that there are also phenomena of alienation in a socialist system. Consequently youth groups with a higher level of education concentrate their political interest and concern on the relationships of the ideal of socialism to the existing social reality.

In the Western democracies few students would interpret their quarrel with society as primarily a generational problem. Certainly, they do not interpret the so-called conflict of the generations as a 'filial' rebellion of an ever-recurring, a-historical kind. Many young people may regard their fathers with less than admiration; on the whole, however, the rebellion of academic youth constitutes, in the eyes of its protagonists, a critique of present-day capitalist society in which the older generation is simply holding the reins of power.

Any merely 'filial' rebellion is made difficult by the fact that in the modern industrial system the family has ceased to play its traditional role. The behavioural pattern of the generational order (comprising grandparents, parents and children) may still persist, but it has lost its normative and regulatory power and taken on an ideological appearance. The modern methods of production or administration are increasingly independent of the age of an individual.[17]

There exists, furthermore, in advanced industrial societies a strong tendency towards the levelling of authority. In a time of rapid social and technological change the ability to learn is valued higher than experience acquired in a lifetime. Family or social structure built entirely on the dignity of age is resented as an attempt to hang on to power. To all this, advanced technology makes its own contribution by emphasising the contemporaneous and simultaneous nature of experience. In the words of a young American, 'I resent being held responsible for not having lived at the time of the depression.'

31

Authority which once was vested in identifiable representatives of the adult generation (such as parents, teachers or priests) has become anonymous as well as internalised. 'Anonymous' suggests that its seat is difficult to locate since it permeates every phase of life, and that visible carriers of functions of authority are easily exchangeable. 'Internalised' means that standards and directions are accepted as if they were one's own decisions, though in reality they are subtly suggested by the managers of the system. Where parental or other educational authority is concerned, 'permissiveness' is the major instrument by which the internalisation of authority is achieved.

This and similar interpretations of 'permissiveness' seem at first sight far-fetched, even preposterous. For 'permissiveness' suggests a liberal and humane pedagogical system, particularly if we compare it with the strict forms of guidance and authority of the past. Such considerations, however, miss the point. For many students interpret 'permissiveness' as a subtle form of repression, typical of the late stages of capitalism. The individual is forced by his own – liberal or sensitised – conscience, which in turn is conditioned by the unexpressed yet ever-present expectations of his elders and of the opinion leaders of his society, to perform in ways that make society function smoothly in the interest of its capitalist owners.

In this sense, the rebellion of youth in the Western democracies may be seen as a curious process within the confines of the late stages of liberalism. It happened at a time when the liberal parents were caught in the apparently insoluble contradictions of the liberal tradition. These contradictions derive, among other things, from the fact that liberalism is on the one hand an expression of the belief in the inalienable rights of man and a perpetual attempt to realise them; on the other hand, it is identified with a historically conditioned economic philosophy, with *laissez-faire*. To the radical young, it is monopolistic capitalism, the heir to *laissez-faire* in our time, that brought technocracy into the world and established the primacy of a well-functioning economic order over human concerns. They dream of the immediate and total realisation of human rights, with the exclusion of the unlimited right to private ownership of the means of production.

As sons and daughters of beneficiaries of the 'liberal' system, they inherited – in addition to greater possibilities of education and to occasional greater wealth – a liberal conscience. And it is this conscience which makes them at times bitter and frustrated critics of their fathers. Parental 'permissiveness' is thus interpreted by the academic young as a well-meaning but ineffectual gesture on the part of their cautious and insecure elders. It seems to them the price their elders are eager to pay to hide their own inability to separate the two main aspects of liberalism, to solve the central problems of the present, to 'humanise' a system which their forefathers created and which by now has come to operate according to its own laws and principles – independently of any sensible human control. This again reinforces the young in their belief that 'permissiveness' is a corollary of repression or, more specifically, of the integration of the individual into an inhuman and self-serving society. In their critique of 'permissiveness' and 'internalisation' radical students accuse the existing socio-economic order in which the interests of its masters are more important than the self-realisation of the great mass of human beings. They are allergic to the 'integration' of individuals and groups into the existing order because it tends to cover up the conflicts of life and in particular the conflicts of interests which are regarded by them as one of the basic themes of social development. In addition, the enforced lack of transparency of issues and conflicts makes participation in decision-making impossible. These factors contribute to what appears at times an extravagantly critical attitude on the part of radical students towards social democracy or progressive education because they interpret them as the most gentle forms of rationalising the dominating system.[18]

A further object of the students' critique – more implied perhaps than overt – is the primacy of the functional intellect. They seem to be convinced that the exclusively intellectual or instrumental element of our mental powers necessarily neglects both the non-intellective awareness (with which hippies and similar groups are concerned) and political consciousness (which the radical students try to develop). Unfortunately, the English language has only one word – 'irrational' – to designate two entirely different phenomena: aversion against the rational and rejection of the purely intellectual. The first connotation may carry with it the idea of a romantic flight from rational and responsible behaviour. The second phenomenon simply pleads against the supremacy of a highly abstract mode of thinking which has its instrumental significance but cannot help us in our search for the proper purposes and directions of our lives. It is against this usurpation of the role of reason by the abstract intellect or, more generally, against the neglect of reason that many young people rebel. This rebellion is a sign of moral and political sensibility, of a humanism which sets the realisation of human rights and possibilities ahead of the interests and ends of an abstract system.

This should explain the fact that the students' revolt is, at most, only at its outer edges a romantic rebellion. If we distinguish between certain by-products of the student revolt – often born out of youthful impatience and simple despair – and the mainstream of protest and renewal, then the principal thrust is in no way romantic. This is no replica of the distinction between the Virgin and the Dynamo, between the mystic culture of the Middle Ages and the mystique of a poorly understood modern world, dominated by the natural sciences. Nor do they repeat the formula of the 'two cultures', one based on the liberal arts, the other on science and technology. It is rather a call for liberating reason (and liberating awareness), for a revival of politics and the arts against the abstract intellect that is simply instrumental and has its goals and directions set by interests and forces not governed by reason.

What critical students aspire to today is well expressed by the German word *Mündigkeit*. Originally, it meant coming of age or reaching majority. It pointed to the privileges and duties of adulthood which were acquired at a certain stage of life. Today *Mündigkeit* is used as a political term, indicating the ability of acquiring for oneself an overview of the important aspects of individual and social life, a grasp of the order of things, and the ability of determining one's own place and tasks.

The young critics of society are keenly aware both of their own lack of *Mündigkeit* within the educational system and the lack of *Mündigkeit* of the overwhelming majority of citizens in our society. Where 'experts' make most of the decisions of detail, it is of vital importance to know whether the co-ordination of these decisions, the determination of the direction in which society is to go, is made by the technocrat and capitalist or by the humanist social reformer or revolutionist. If *Mündigkeit* is a general social

34

and political goal for today's radical youth, then some of the definitions and interpretations of 'youth' or of the 'conflict of generations' are automatically disqualified. We have mentioned already the concept of 'filial generation', of youth being defined as a reaction to the older generation.

It is here that the distinction between today's youth and previous youth movements, for example the German youth movement after the First World War, becomes clear. In the twenties the prime opponent was one's own family and its style of life, while today it is the whole of middle-class society. Then, if we again take the German case, youth sought a solution for youth – in a separate realm, unsullied by any adult presence. Today, youth is concerned with the problems of the world. Some of these problems – like war and misdirected or substandard education – may affect youth more than adults. But the causes of these and many other problems are seen by many young people as the outgrowth of systems and institutions that, it is true, are usually governed by older people; this, however, cannot hide the fact that the adult is as much the victim of those systems and institutions as is youth and that youth tries to liberate man regardless of his age.

Of course, there exists a number of interpretations which try to belittle the importance of today's youth. Some of the older liberals in America, for example, see the radicals of today simply as the children of the 'Old Left' of the 1930s, and the silent generation of the 1950s as the children of the conservative decade of the 1920s. Others state that there is no generation gap, since the voting patterns in recent elections in America and England show that certain differences in voting *within* the younger generation were greater than those *between* the older and younger generations. At the same time, some of the radical students suspect that the adult members of their society use and emphasise the category 'youth' in order to reduce the problem of *Mündigkeit*, which affects the whole of society, to a mere problem of youth, that is to say, of youthful immaturity. Werner Loch may be closer to the truth when he writes : 'The great revolution in the relationship of the generations consists in the fact that the moral consciousness of society which heretofore had been traditionally conceded to be a part of the older generation, is kept awake by youth. . . . The work of Sisyphus, "to keep awake the consciousness" (Camus),

35

has been taken over by youth. This is the secret meaning of their revolt.'[19]

In addition to treating the general social criticism of youth as a specific phenomenon of its natural immaturity, society has found another, probably more effective way of taking the sting out of young people's attacks. It consists in giving the lack of *Mündigkeit* characteristic of youth a positive meaning and making of it an acceptable ideal for the whole of society. The ideal of youth and youthfulness, of being free of cares and responsibilities, of taking life as entertainment and play, is being propagated incessantly by the mass media. It is an effective way of integrating youth and the older adherents of the ideal of youthfulness into a system of production and consumption which politically conscious youth regards as its prime enemy.

One of the most controversial aspects of the student movement is its often strong utopian quality. It is particularly here that critics believe they detect a desire to escape the complex industrial world to which the student of the humanities and of the social sciences is allegedly unwilling to adjust. Thus he either returns in hippy fashion to the 'simple life' of the rural community or advocates the sudden and violent realisation of a proletarian society. Critics point out that the fulfilment of such a utopia, a world without rules, without any form of rulership, would signify the destruction of all political freedom,[20] since freedom implies the rational division of tasks, functions and responsibilities as well as the consent of the governed. The students' utopia is criticised further as being a 'weapon of romantic and utopian criticism of modern society'[21] rather than an instrument in its progressive transformation. It 'neglects reform and propagates total destruction as a path towards emancipation'.[22] Finally, it betrays the 'critical function of intellectuals – to seek the truth rather than to pretend to have found it'.[23] Each of these criticisms touches upon some point of the vast spectrum of student revolt; none does justice to the movement as a whole. Remembering the necessity of distinguishing the two basic meanings of the word 'irrational', we see in much of the student movements not a romantic return to an irrational utopia, an escape from today's reality, but, as in all true revolutionary thought, a return to the rational, and therefore timeless, principles of natural law and a desire to act upon it according to the needs of our time. Observers politically as far apart as Hannah Arendt and Ernst Bloch see in the student revolt a basically moral motivation. More precisely, they believe that it draws inspiration from the ideas of the late eighteenth century, from the trust in natural law. At the same time, we recognise a note of despair in what might easily be the last attempt in the history of Western civilisation to initiate a humanist revolution. 'Behind the renewal of radical hope', writes Hannah Arendt,[24] lurks 'a basic element of despair. In American and in Western Europe we see a despair in them as if they knew that they will be crushed.'

One could here ask whether their notion that technology *could* furnish the basis of the satisfaction of the needs of *all* people on earth is utopian in a reprehensible sense? Or whether they are escapists because they dare to hope and act despite the negative prognosis of any calculus of the probability of success? Perhaps those unknown individuals were right who during the Paris uprisings in May 1968 wrote on the walls of the Sorbonne 'Let us be realists! Let us demand the impossible!' – because, indeed, within the realm of what men of the world regard as possible there are no chances for the young – or for the world.

At the same time one should not forget that the rebellion of radical students, particularly in the Western world, is no doubt also based on an interest of class. The rebellious sons and daughters of liberal parents find their status as humanists endangered by the rapid growth of technology which may prevent them from finding a place for themselves in an automatised and strictly functional society. Already in school and, to a higher degree, in the universities, some of them find an atmosphere which is quite different from the liberal and permissive tone characteristic of their own families.

In tracing the student revolt of recent years we find that a term frequently used for the enemy was 'repression'. It was the term that for many related the woes of the university to the woes of society. For repression in the universities was thought to reflect faithfully repression in the society at large. In similar fashion, the struggle against a repressive educational system was regarded as a necessary condition for a successful fight against the social system. But also the reverse was thought to be true: only the liberation of society from repression was able to grant the conditions for education towards freedom in the home, the school and the university. Repression, of course, appeared in different forms in the liberal Western democracies, in the Eastern socialist countries and on the Iberian Peninsula.

In Spain the students' struggle was directed against an oppressive regime which seriously restricted the students' right to assemble, summarily dismissed professors who demanded reform of the university structure, and ordered or condoned the ruthless intervention of police in the universities. In Prague, where students were well aware of the strong democratic traditions that had preceded the advent of the Communist regime, they had used the historical student May Day celebrations as occasions of protest against police brutality, the tendentious information given to them about the Soviet Union, and the general censorship. Finally, in Yugoslavia, where the majority of the students accepted the projected goals of a socialist society, repression was identified with the older generation of politicians and with a hierarchical university system that had hardly been modified since the days of the Austro-Hungarian Empire. In most of the other countries of the Eastern bloc, but particularly in the Soviet Union, students were so completely integrated in the university system, which demanded from each of them the highest possible measure of performance, that only a few dissident individuals were willing and able to raise their voice.

STAGES OF STUDENT DISSATISFACTION

In the liberal West there exists a whole gamut of reasons for student dissatisfaction. Some of the student ideologists believe they see three stages in the reaction to this situation. A first stage, covering the period from 1960 to 1965, is said to have shown a growing political interest which was limited, however, to specific aspects of the students' life such as housing and meals or to blatant offences on the part of the authorities against the basic democratic order. A second stage which culminated in the commotions and confrontations of the years 1968 and 1969 was represented by the anti-authoritarian struggle. It has been followed by a third stage which is outwardly more quiet and is characterised on the one hand by frustration and despair, and on the other by small-group action both of an ideological and a social-cum-practical nature.

The student ideologists alluded to see as part of the first phase the expression of solidarity by some French students for an Algerian student who had been dismissed from the university (1962); the protest by French students against the censorship and suppression of student and secondary school newspapers (1965); the demonstrations against the raising of streetcar fares in Austria (1965); and the actions against the lack of dormitory facilities and the overcrowding of seminars at German universities. Concerning the suppression of democratic liberties in foreign countries, Germany alone experienced in 1961 demonstrations of protest against the murder of Lumumba; in 1962 an attempt to make a collection for Algerian refugees (which was forbidden by the Rector of the Berlin Free University); in 1963 a sit-down strike in Munich to demonstrate the students' solidarity with the leaders of the American black community; in 1964 protest demonstrations against the visit of Moïse Tshombe; in 1965) protest actions against a propaganda week for South Africa, and the first large anti-Vietnam war demonstration.

Most of the young activists, no doubt, did not find the opportunities open to them in the existing social service organisations or political parties to their liking. Only a few countries make provisions for constructive social service on a large scale. (One may think of Sweden and her tradition of letting young men serve in international organisations like the United Nations peacekeeping force.) In the political realm, many young people are aware of the unattractiveness of the traditional democratic parties. The sections for younger members, particularly of the liberal and social-democratic parties, generally resent the rule of seniority and the general 'establishment' character of the mother parties. In Germany they have either been expelled for their radical behaviour or have left the respective parties of their own accord. In England the 'May Day Manifesto' of 1967 was an indictment of the Labour Party's participation in the managed politics of technocratic capitalism.[25] In Italy the Centre-Left coalition was seen as an attempt at integrating the socialist parties into the existing system.

As far as the universities and the teaching staffs are concerned, the students have a long list of grievances. They believe that the existing structure of the institutions of higher learning and the concept of science represented by them are neither relevant to a critical analysis of the society in which they live nor to the students' professional preparation. We have mentioned before that in a rapidly changing world, with a high rate of growth of information and of development of new techniques, authority based on age and experience is less important than the continuing ability to learn. Students therefore reject the traditional hierarchical structure of the universities, corresponding as they do to the medieval productive unit of master, journeyman and apprentice. The professor is seen as the master who is holding an impregnable position from which he is able to make what appears to the student as arbitrary decisions affecting not only his studies but also his future. In particular, students rebel against the selection of material presented in lectures or asked of students in examinations, since it often reflects the immediate research interests of a professor rather than the interest or needs of a student. Students protest with particular vehemence against the lack of opportunity of entering into critical discussions with their professors. One must add that even where personal relations between professors and students have once existed – though Continental universities have never enjoyed the benefit of tutorials and residential colleges – these are now increasingly hampered by the growth of the student body and by the reticence on the part of universities and professors to give up the chair-system. This system means, at least in the Continental countries, that there is generally only one chair for each academic subject (today there may be two or three chairs in subjects with several thousands of students) rather than a department with a large teaching staff.

At the same time, there is a strong reaction on the part of students against university administrations which make their decisions in ways that are neither public nor otherwise transparent. Of the three types of decisions that are of interest to students – those by Ministries of Education, those by university administrations and those by the faculties or the university senates – the latter are physically closest and come first under attack. The chief purpose of the students was, and is, to force the decision-making process into the open and to be represented in more than token fashion on the governing bodies. One can probably generalise and say that most student riots and general unrest occurred where a specific event provided an opportunity for combining the anti-authoritarian bias against a university measure with an anti-authoritarian bias against society in general.

A special case is represented by the long history of clashes at two of the most liberal universities in the Western world, at the University of California at Berkeley and the Free University in West Berlin. In both places the respective university administrations seem to have been unaware of how sensitive students had become to the problem of their rights as individuals in the face of an increasingly impersonal university apparatus. An issue which in former times would probably have been overlooked sparked a revolt which set the different elements of the academic community against each other. At Berkeley it was the limitation of free assembly and speech in an area of the campus traditionally reserved for it which in 1964 led to the 'Free Speech Movement', in 1966 to a student strike and in 1969 to the brutal clearing by police of the so-called 'People's Park'. In Berlin it was the suppression of a student campaign by the Academic Senate, a suppression that was in turn backed by the city government, the throwing of a bomb against an anti-Vietnam discussion meeting at the Technical University, the breaking up by police of a sit-down strike before the Amerika-Haus, and the prohibition by the Academic Senate of all political meetings in university buildings.

In Belgium it was the language and culture conflict between Flemings and Walloons which absorbed most of the students' political energies; in Paris it was the crowding of the universities and their antiquated structure but also the limitations imposed upon male and female students concerning visits in student homes of the opposite sex which led to demonstrations; in Prague the quality of the student dining-halls and dormitories; in Vienna the introduction of a new method of statistical analysis of students. In Bonn students demonstrated in order to ask that the title of honorary senator of the university be taken away from the President of the Republic. In Bremen and other German and Austrian cities thousands of students and secondary-school pupils marched against the raising of the price for public transport.

Already in 1966 students had demonstrated in Berlin and Frankfurt against the war in Vietnam. Similar demonstrations occurred in the following two or three years in many European cities. In 1967 the S.D.S. (the German Socialist Student Union) decided upon the permanent university revolt after its offices had been searched by police. In June of that year a demonstration was held in Berlin against the state visit of the Shah of Persia during which a student was shot and killed by police. A wave of protest followed in practically all German universities. Further demonstrations were held against the military regime in Greece and against the concentration of the Berlin Press in the hands of the Springer publishing house, which was accused of actively nourishing the animosity of the population against the students. Shortly before Easter 1968 an attempt was made on the life of the radical student leader Rudi Dutschke; this was followed by riots in several cities. In many universities, institutes and administrative offices were occupied and lectures disturbed.

IDEOLOGICAL INFLUENCES

At this point we must ask who were the ideological mentors, who the personal examples, and who the tactical leaders of the student revolt which gathered force in 1967 and reached its climax in 1968. Most of the mentors were, characteristically, of an advanced age: Ho Chi Minh, Mao Tse-tung, Herbert Marcuse. Theirs, so it seems, was the wisdom of the grandfathers purged, as it were, of any repressive trait that might be characteristic of the generation of the fathers. Ho Chi Minh and Mao Tse-tung were, at the same time, living examples; in this capacity they were joined by men like Fidel Castro, Che Guevara, and by some of the leaders of revolutionary groups such as the Black Panthers. What they had in common was that they were personalities dedicated to the creation of a co-operative, socialist and non-bureaucratic type of society. With the exception of the Black Panthers they operated in close-to-feudalistic peasant milieus which were exploited by Western free enterprise aided by political and economic colonialism. The Black Panthers were fascinating precisely because they tried to carry the tactics of the Third World revolutionary movements into the urban ghettos. The radical students, by identifying themselves with the leaders in the struggle against colonial or neo-colonial rule, abandoned in a sense their own middle-class environment with its apparently insoluble problems to join, at least in thought, the Robin Hoods of their time.

Their own leaders, the Savios, Dutschkes, Cohn-Bendits, were of little more than tactical importance. The mass media played them up in order to make the student movement dramaturgically viable – by creating 'heroes' and 'villains'. These 'leaders' were most likely both product and personification of movements which in their anti-authoritarian phase were in honour bound to debunk their own leaders as soon as they had brought them to the fore. Few of them, if any, were revolutionary types capable of grasping power or likely to know what to do with it. Most of them were soon ready to return to the amenities of private life, some with the conviction that spontaneous action was not an efficient way of winning over larger parts of the population.

If one tries to locate ideologically the various trends and groupings within the student movement, one is struck by the fact that practically all radical student groups orient themselves along one or the other interpretation of Marx or the Marxist tradition. One of the major reasons appears to be that dialectical materialism is seen as the only available scientific-redemptive method, an Archimedean point, which allows one to grasp the world in its present structure and contradictions and lift it out of its position. We have already seen that radical students regard the sciences taught in the traditional universities as irrelevant to their purpose of gaining insight into the true working of reality and, in particular, of social reality. Without a clear understanding of these workings, a student or graduate will flounder before his own conscience and be a pawn within the impenetrable machinations of the big and little powers of this world. Positivism, the discovery and abstract ordering of facts, supposedly without regard to any value orientation, will not allow him to relate the given world to his search for meaning; nor will neo-humanistic idealism make of the values of the past effective guidelines for the solution of individual or social problems of the present. It is Marxism which suggests to radical youth the possibility of stripping the veil of peaceful integration from the true contradictions of social and economic life, and the faith that scientific analysis in the manner of dialectical materialism will by itself provide the categories and directions of progressive (or revolutionary) social action.

Many Marxist students are aware of the fact that the prediction of Marx that the increase in productivity would ring in a reign of freedom has been disproved by the fact that the higher the productivity of society the greater the enslavement of the individual to the needs which the system must create in order to perpetuate itself. Most of today's radical students reject modern industrial society both in its Western-capitalist and in its Soviet-communist form. They repudiate their crude materialism, their bureaucratic organisation, and the purely instrumental character of the respective forms of rationality.

Grossly oversimplifying, one can speak during the anti-authoritarian phase of two major types of reaction to this situation. One group tended to vent their frustration with the East European socialist regimes through identification with one or other of the charismatic leaders of violence. For violence can be rationalised both as absolute negation (of a world which is difficult to grasp and still more difficult to transform) and absolute affirmation, for him who sets loyalty to an absolute leader ahead of loyalty to an absolute idea. This implies a change in the traditional interpretation of class in the direction of the ideas of Frantz Fanon or Régis Debray. According to Debray, the proletariat are not the workers in the tin mines of Bolivia or the peasants who are in a similar way bound to their place of work and to the defence of their own interests, but the guerrillas who are at all times victims of the hazards of the revolution. Radical students see an analogy between their own situation and that of the guerrillas in the Third World: they are not bound, like a labourer, to a fixed place of work, and the interests they defend are not those of the students alone. Revolution to them is the anticipated notion of a common 'existential' experience, the anticipation of utopia as the final cause of all human worth (and in some countries perhaps a substitute for the partisan experience that their elders had during the last war).

A second group of students expresses the belief that, among other things, it was primarily the neglect of psychology and of the struggle against individual and social-psychic repression that prevented the hoped-for socialist paradise from being realised. They try to find a reconciliation of the Marxian and Freudian traditions, corresponding to the enhancement of political consciousness and of aesthetic awareness. In addition to Wilhelm Reich, the most influential mentor of these attempts was the German-American philosopher and student of metapsychology, Herbert Marcuse. He interpreted aesthetics on one hand as 'pertaining to art', on the other hand as 'pertaining to the senses'. As to art, he took up Friedrich Schiller's concept of aesthetic education, 'which would serve to transform the repressive political order into one of freedom and instinctual fulfilment'. 'The opposition between imagination and reason . . . poetic and scientific thought, would be invalidated.'[26] In between the traditional conception of art and the realm of life which Marcuse identifies as the object of psychoanalytical study in the tradition of Freud lies the field of an undefined 'new sensibility' which together with an equally undefined 'new rationality' is the basis for the radical transformation of society. 'The new sensibility has become a political factor.'[27] Marcuse was more precise when he tried to reconcile Marxism (presumably the source of the 'new consciousness') with Freudian psychoanalysis (presumably the source of the 'new sensibility'). He believed, together with other Freudian radicals, that sexual pleasure was the ultimate measure of human happiness, and that sexual repression was characteristic of modern civilisation – in fact, that it was one of the principal mechanisms of political domination.[28]

Under capitalism, 'love became a matter of duty and habit, carefully circumscribed by the ideology of monogamic fidelity. Its sole function, beyond perpetuating the species, was the hygienic one of maintaining the physical and mental health necessary to the continued functioning of the economic apparatus.'[29] 'He argued that in a society where all value is based on labour, pleasure was necessarily devalued. . . . "The unsublimated, unrationalised release of sexual relations would mean the most emphatic release of pleasure as such and the total devaluation of work for work's sake." ' Marcuse speaks of 'repressive desublimation' or 'repressive tolerance' as typical of the 'permissiveness' of liberal civilisation. 'The fact that sex has been incorporated into the workaday world contributes to the voluntary compliance of the repressed individual with the regulations and goals of the repressive order.'[30]

In *Eros and Civilisation* (1955) Marcuse was convinced 'that the new erotic order would represent such a radical departure from the world of the performance principle that work itself would assume a new character of play relations, and he even suggested that work might become a form of erotic release . . .'[31] However, after *One-Dimensional Man* (1964) and 'Political Preface 1966' (to *Eros and Civilisation*), he proclaimed his disillusionment with the classical Marxist prognosis that the advance of industrialisation itself would eventually lead to freedom. He felt that he had overestimated the revolutionary potential of advanced industrial society and that the sexual revolution had been betrayed.[32] As a consequence, he advocated 'absolute refusal' as the only legitimate political posture. He started to doubt whether it was still possible to 'speak of a juncture between the erotic and political dimensions. In and against the deadly efficient organisation of the affluent society, not only radical protest, but even the attempts to formulate, to articulate, to give word to protest assumes a childlike, ridiculous immaturity.'[33]

The specific intellectual or ideological development of the politically active parts of the student body was, of course, different in different countries. In the Federal Republic of Germany, for example, Sartre, Camus but also Freud were widely read before the onset of the radicalisation in 1966–7. Around 1967–8 Adorno and Habermas, leaders of the Frankfurt school of sociology, reintroduced Marxism, modified, as in Marcuse's case, by their stay in the United States, into Germany. 1969–70 saw again a return to orthodox Marxism and a rejection by many students of the transformations that it had suffered at the hands of the Frankfurt school. Generally, we can say that Germany was handicapped in its reception of Marxism by several events: the exclusion of Marx from the German scene during the Third Reich and in the period of reconstruction immediately following the war; the preoccupation with the question of war-guilt in the fifties and sixties; the discrediting of leftist movements through Stalinism; the anti-Communism of the Cold War period; and a specifically German belief in the possibility of constructing philosophical systems without much regard to common-sense experience.

3. STUDENT UNREST IN VARIOUS COUNTRIES

In England one of the ideologically interested groups published the monthly *Solidarity*. It stressed the idea that a revolutionary organisation of socialists must be decentralised in order to mirror the structure of the future society of workers' councils. Another group published the weekly *Socialist Worker* which represented positions from semi-anarchist to orthodox Trotskyite and served the primary purpose of socialist education among workers. In general, it was the Maoist and particularly the Trotskyite positions that were most widely accepted by the ideologically interested part of the younger generation. In France there occurred the formation of new groups such as the Strasbourg commune of the 'situationists' which originated out of a disillusionment with the older groups on the Left. Their manifesto about poverty, borrowing from Bakunin and Reich, advocated the spontaneous satisfaction of needs (for example, by stealing).

The actual political events differed from country to country, among other things, because of the relative weight of the anti-authoritarian struggle and the desire for participatory democracy. In countries like Germany where the structure of the universities and, to a great extent, of society had traditionally been quite rigid, the anti-authoritarian struggle stood in the foreground. In countries like France where, next to a centralised state machine, the traditions of revolutionary participation were still alive, or in the Netherlands, Great Britain or the Scandinavian countries, where direct participation in local government had long been a matter of course, the desire for a new and different type of more 'relevant' participation found strong expression.

Where participation was emphasised, both as far as the universities and society at large were concerned, it meant considerably more than being present at the making of decisions, more even than exerting a certain control over their outcome. Participation as an expression of *Mündigkeit* was thought to imply a qualitative change : from a merely functional or instrumental aspect of partaking in decisions to decisions of a subjective or existential kind. For 'Youth demands a world which makes sense, which is founded on reason, or failing that, on a mystique'.[34] This desire for participation in organs of the university or of society often went hand in hand with radical criticism or even total rejection.

In England there was remarkably little of outright student revolt.[35] The most exciting events occurred outside the universities. In October 1968 about 100,000 people marched in London under the banner 'Victory to the N.L.F. (Vietnamese National Liberation Front) and to the Vietnamese Revolution !' Most of them were probably under the impression that they were demonstrating against the capitalist system.[36] (By the time of the 1969 Vietnam mobilisation the number of marchers had shrunk to only a few thousand.)

During the Algerian war, and particularly between 1961 and 1962, and during the Indo-China war (1954) the French National Student Union had played a strong oppositional role, though it was often handicapped by the Communist Party which tried to identify itself more with national than with class interests. The strongest student reaction was probably provoked in 1964–5 by the Fouché Plan which contemplated a decidedly technocratic university reform. The reform planned by Edgar Faure (Minister of Education until the formation of the Chaban-Delmas Government) was also based on the tradition of a centralised university system which had been inherited from the kings of France and adopted and developed by the Revolution, the Empire and the Republics.[37] The revolt in May 1968 had, then, a number of causes : Nanterre constituted a university ghetto with no normal recreational outlets; it had been planned by a centralised state; most important of all, there existed a deep-seated conviction among students concerning the crisis of contemporary Western civilisation and 'a rejection of everything as it exists now'.[38] Significantly, the forces which took part in the revolt represented a multiplicity of tendencies. The most tangible result, according to the students, was the complete destruction of the authority of professors and teachers.

Politically alert Italian students[39] claimed to reject affluence, particularly in its Americanised forms. They were furthermore intensely aware of the archaic structure and rigidity of the Italian state, including its universities (one could call it the material of their frustration) and of the international movements – in Vietnam, Latin America and China (which were taken as models for thought and action). At the university they were caught in the process of transition from an institution created for a social elite to a mass institution – an ambivalent situation since they themselves were by social origin members of an elite but wanted to play a new role of leadership based not on origin or social interest but on a more highly developed political consciousness and on the idea of being of service to all progressive forces in the country. As in France, also in Italy the new radicalism was rooted in Marxism, often seen, as in Germany, through an American prism, particularly through the interpretation of Marcuse. Generally, one can speak of two larger groupings : the anti-repressive, anti-technocratic moderate Left, and the radical Left which tried to use methods and experiences of the politically advanced students in the service of socially underprivileged and politically still inarticulate groups. The second group, in particular, advocated permanent agitation. In this they were unintentionally helped by the repressive measures undertaken by academic authorities and police which awakened feelings of solidarity among normally uncommitted students.

Didactically, politically alert students favoured group discussions as a first phase in the process of political education, as a first form of relief from internalised repression and from the kind of individualistic deformation which tends to inhibit creative and socially useful life. Organisationally, the model for the University of Turin may serve as an example of a more general tendency. Two concurrent reforms were here contemplated : one referred to the official teaching and research mechanisms in the established university, the other to an autonomous, politically structured division which was tolerated to exist within the gates of the official institution.

ATTEMPTS AT SOLIDARITY

The student movement, particularly in its more spectacular phase, undertook numerous attempts at stepping beyond the walls of the academic ghetto. Marxist thought had taught students to see in the working class the prime revolutionary potential which, where it had not yet become conscious of the decisive role that the logic of history had prepared for it, had to be enlightened by the politically conscious elite, the radical students.

The success of the various attempts to achieve solidarity with the workers was nowhere spectacular. The degree of indifference or even hostility did not depend primarily on the social system. In industrially advanced countries of all types the average worker was conservative. He intended to fight for a larger slice of the Gross National Product while doing everything in his power to protect the political and economic system against all disturbing influences, be they enemies from without or students with un-conventional behaviour, not to speak of revolutionary ideologies. On a number of occasions members of the working class expressed their hate against the disrupting tactics of radical students. At Berlin in February 1968 a student demonstration against the Vietnam war was countered by a demonstration of workers, organised by the Senate of the city and a number of large indus-trial plants, in support of the foreign policy of the United States. During the same year student unrest in Yugoslavia brought forth protest meetings in several factories at which the rebellious students were indicted as counter-revolutionaries. Less than 1 per cent of the Yugoslav population is said to have supported the student demands.

In countries like Spain or Portugal the situation was more complex. Under the common experience of an oppressive regime, *comissiones obreras*, mixed groups of students, workers and priests, had existed for years. In the Basque provinces, the most highly industrialised part of Spain, such committees were com-posed of two-thirds of workers and one-third of students. Yet both students and workers considered their co-operation as little more than a tactical measure : the students wanted to lead their struggle independently of any popular front conception; the workers, in turn, nourished a historical distrust against the student sons and daughters of the middle class.

In France and Italy, where Communist Parties had long been established as an important political force, students had tried to attract their attention. The result was usually mutual disappointment and recrimination. Radical students in Italy rather sympathise with dissident Communist groups which were suspended or expelled from the official party and follow an anti-Soviet, Trotskyite and pro-Chinese line. In Paris parallel activities of students and workers, if not an actual alliance, had taken place in May 1968. The reasons for this extraordinary event were probably several. One may think of a momentary coincidence of grievances, of a long and common tradition harking back to the French Revolution, of an extraordinarily intelligent and politically sophisticated proletariat, and of the respect of the common man for the cultural and intellectual 'elite'.

In Yugoslavia student unrest expressed itself in June 1968 particularly at the universities of Belgrade and Zagreb. The journal *The Student* wrote: 'Why do students demonstrate? . . . First of all, they demand the attenuation of the great social inequalities in our society; that the problem of unemployment be solved and that our workers need not emigrate to foreign countries; that real democracy be assured in all areas of social life.' Another document, 'The Belgrade Students' Programme of Political Action', asked that the process of democratisation be hastened, particularly in the League of Communists:

'All mass media should be thoroughly democratised and constitutional liberties and rights ensured in that area . . . The University should be organised as a self-governing institution at which progressive scientific thought can be developed freely . . . It is particularly necessary to ensure the real participation of students in self-government . . . Measures must be taken to ensure that the social structure of the student body correspond to the social structure of society as a whole . . . We ask for a stronger influence of science, of the University and of the students in the formulation of ways, forms and methods for our further social and economic development . . . Concerning the personnel policy of the University, it is necessary to do away with tenure for all positions and to open the University to all young people who are capable of research and pedagogical work.'

During the anti-authoritarian phase, violence against objects and occasionally also against persons was part of the struggle. In Stephen Spender's words, 'acutely conscious of the transitoriness of their unique situation, [students] feel that they must "do something" . . . without paying undue respect to due process . . . Their positive beliefs are in social justice and social salvation rather than in the order favoured by so many of their elders.'[40]

Radical student groups liked to impair the functioning of decision-making bodies as long as their basic demands for operation in public and student participation were not satisfied. Thus, in the most extreme cases, offices of deans were broken into, faculty meetings were invaded by hundreds of students, microphones were pulled out of the hands of professors and lectures changed by the use of force into general assemblies. Democratic participation was at times identified with plebiscitarian democracy which, in turn, was thought to guarantee *eo ipso* the rational character of its decisions. 'Anti-universities' were planned *outside* the existing institutions (the 'diggers', for example, an anarchist group which takes its name from the radical sect of the seventeenth century, attempted such a counter- or anti-institution early in 1968 in London); *within* the universities sections entirely planned and run by students were inaugurated as 'critical' or 'free' universities. At the same time, student couples with young children who believed that anti-authoritarian education and agitation had to start with the child, struggled to organise nursery schools for pre-school children which were to be free from any form of repression or sublimation. Some took their children to lectures and other university events where they let them 'do their thing' without inhibition.

An important issue arose of course from the fact that radical students constituted a political elite, or, as the statisticians would say, a relatively small minority of the total student population. To this one must add that in West European and to a certain extent also in East European countries, middle- and upper-middle-class families furnish a disproportionately high number of students while the working classes – industrial workers and peasants – are under-represented.

A most striking example is Spain where after the Civil War only the sons and daughters of higher officers, of the upper-middle class, and of higher civil servants attended university. During the last fifteen years the middle section of the middle class has furnished most of the students. Only less than 1 per cent of the student body comes from the working classes. Recent Yugoslav statistics show that at the University of Zagreb 10.6 per cent of students come from agricultural homes, the fathers of 3.7 per cent of students are unskilled labourers, and 48.4 per cent of the students have fathers with higher education. As far as Yugoslav secondary schools are concerned, 29 per cent of male and 37 per cent of female pupils attending commercial schools come from an agricultural environment; in the more academic secondary schools (leading to permission to attend university) they are only 2 and 4 per cent, while the greatest attendance comes from children whose fathers are academics or civil servants. In the Federal Republic of Germany the percentage of university students whose fathers are civil servants has declined between 1967 and 1970 from approximately one-third to one-quarter of the student body, while the percentage of students from working-class or peasant homes has climbed from 6 to 10 per cent.

Among the students attending university, again only a small percentage are political activists. The American psychiatrist Kenneth Keniston thinks that only 2 per cent of the age group can be described as radical youth. In Germany one assumes that roughly 3 per cent of the student body are consistently activists. They are dedicated and disciplined and were able, at least during the anti-authoritarian phase, to mobilise many thousands of students who had heretofore minded their own business and shown only mild pleasure in the difficulties that by then had become the daily bread of academic and political authorities. A necessary condition for the momentary activation of the latent solidarity of the apolitical majority of the students was always an occasion which also offended their sense of justice.

An opinion poll taken in the Federal Republic of Germany during the anti-authoritarian phase of the student revolt indicated that 80 per cent of all students were in favour of considerable changes in the social and political situation, while 75 per cent of the general population were against it. Another poll asked pupils and students whether they approved of young people protesting and demonstrating in German cities. 71 per cent of pupils at secondary schools and 74 per cent of university students answered in the affirmative. 64 per cent of pupils and 67 per cent of students said that they were themselves ready to demonstrate. At the same time, only between 30 and 40 per cent of German students took part in balloting for representatives in the student parliaments.

The anti-authoritarian phase of the student movement lasted only one or two years. The radical students soon learned from bitter experience that their spontaneous and improvised actions were not likely to bring the system down. Also, in the exuberance of the moment they had overestimated their forces. A long-range revolutionary strategy did not exist and was difficult to develop.

THE BREAK-UP OF UNITY

With the end of the immediacy of action came the break-up of a degree of unity which during the anti-authoritarian or participatory phase had held the most diverse student groups together. Frustrated about the future, some former political activists withdrew into the primarily aesthetic 'alternative culture'. Others who had previously despised any action that might help in mending or ameliorating the existing system (since this would prolong its life) decided to undertake acts of social service on behalf of underprivileged groups while continuing, in their own small circles, attempts at ideological clarification. Some even entered the more progressive democratic parties in the hope of getting a chance at some form of political influence. Again others became the victims of complete apathy.

A considerable number of radical students tried to concentrate upon a thorough study of the basic Marxist texts. Of these one group – which in Germany operates under the name of 'red cells' – reminds one of the attitude of fundamentalist sects. They believe that the understanding of the master's work and of the works of his major disciples will one day set them free. While the 'red cells' aim at the modification and reinforcement of the political consciousness of their members, another group, composed of Spartacists and Trotskyites, attempts to build up political cadres. This group hopes eventually to attract workers also and to become an alternative to the official Communist Parties. Finally, there are the so-called workers' basis groups which still hold on to the idea that the workers are potentially the revolutionary class. It is the task of the students to awaken their class-consciousness which is at present dormant. To this end some students detach themselves from university politics in order to work in industrial plants where they concentrate their attention primarily on apprentices.

As far as political action within the universities is concerned, the second phase of ideological preparation is outwardly considerably quieter than the previous phase of confrontation. The chief place of operation is no longer the university as a whole or the large lecture hall but a university institute or school, and within an institute, the individual seminar. Here radical students try to build up small cells which, in addition to the study of Marxist texts, try to infiltrate politically the place of work where the real decisions of academic life, of teaching and research, are being made. The work of an institute, once presided over by a senior scholar, is to be organised along lines of equal representation of the interested parties: one-third students, one-third teaching assistants, one-third professors. In addition, some seminars are to be held exclusively by students according to the dictum of the identity of those who teach and those who learn.

4. CONCLUSION

If we now attempt to assess the effects and the effectiveness of the youth movements and in particular of the student revolt, we must distinguish between general, relatively intangible aspects and concrete consequences in various fields of life. Considering the general significance of the youth movements, one can probably say that the great divide today does not lie, as it did in the nineteenth century, between classes or, as many of us may have thought until recently, between races, but between an aesthetic awareness and critical, political consciousness on one side and a certain obtuseness on the other side. In this sense, the youth movements, including the student revolt, represent only the visible part of an iceberg, the most spectacular form of articulation of a world-wide historical process. Of concrete consequences we see, first of all, the effect of the youth culture and of the student revolt on pre-university youth. In France, a recent study[41] of two *lycées* has shown that the traditional apolitical attitude of the pupils has given way to keen political interest. In 1963 the author of the study encountered only feeble interest; today he believes he sees 'a new manner of being young'. By the end of 1964 he simply observed that 'the great majority of pupils are hostile to the government'. During the summer of 1968, however, a typical statement of a pupil read: 'Socialism, for me, is my ideal; that is all.' At the same time the author notes a deep dissatisfaction of the pupils with their school. He writes: 'The student revolt permitted, in fact, the pupils in the *lycées* to transfer their scholastic dissatisfaction to the plane of society as a whole. The contrast between the values which they have been taught and the values implied in reality has been underlined by the spectacle of the world: the unequal social conditions in France, the wars in Vietnam and Biafra, the problem of the blacks in the wealthiest of nations, the United States.' Asked how they believe they can achieve a socialist society, some pupils answered: 'Through revolution. The revolution is above all the triumph of morality, the end of the realm of money . . . it is, first of all, the end of that passive and unbalanced existence which one has lived (so far) in the scholastic ghettos . . . There is the solidarity with one's comrades . . . against the forces of an 'order' which is nothing but an institutionalised disorder.'

One of the *lycées* studied is situated in a working-class district, the other in a middle-class metropolitan area. For working-class pupils the problem of the future turns primarily around the job; they do not denounce society as absurd but as unjust. It is not consumption that is scandalous but that so few consume so much and so great a mass of people so little. 'Two schools, two mentalities. But those who find the world absurd and those who find it unjust – will they be able to join forces?' One thing only is certain – that the age group attending the *lycées* 'is more numerous, better schooled, more urbanised, more consuming than their elders'.

In society at large, the French study outlines, competition is still the law of life, as failure is regarded as a personal fault. Excellence 'expressed itself not only as the victory of intelligence over imbecility, but also as the triumph of virtue over vice'. Now, however, we see the first generation of adolescents who reject that idea of guilt. It means that the forces which customarily had been absorbed by individual competition are now free for the world-wide confrontation between what Marx calls the 'totally free man' and those who 'utilise spiritual values in order to maintain the value of value, that is to say, [the rule of] money'.

A related question, namely, what role today's secondary school students will play once they enter the universities, is as difficult to answer as the more general question as to what effect the student revolt will in the long run have upon the institutions of higher learning. So far we can observe two contradictory tendencies: on the one hand, certain attempts at reform; on the other hand, a reaction to the student revolt in the form of a consolidation of the more conservative forces in society and on the part of the state itself.

Regarding the attempts at reform which have so far been made in a number of countries, one thing seems certain: the bulk of the energy that ministries and university administrations have expended has been related to rising enrolments. In other words, the major part of the increase in expenditure has been used to enlarge the capacity of existing universities and to create new institutions. Furthermore, the bulk of additional money and a large part of the attention have gone to subjects which prepare students more or less directly for a specific job. Purely humanistic subjects, studies which by their very nature should deal with the problems that ail our world (and consequently constitute the major causes of the student rebellion), are being largely neglected. To this one must add that most of the reforms that have been realised so far refer to administrative matters. More important still is the fact that the majority of the problems which are being debated by the decision-making bodies in which students participate are not related to the central issues – the problem of inter-human relations, the *Mündigkeit* of the students, the priority of social concerns over matters of strictly administrative character.

There are universities like Bergen in Norway where a token representation of students has existed since its foundation in 1948; there are other universities, for example in Germany, where the elected president comes from the ranks of the junior lecturers or where students and junior lecturers have a majority of the votes in the higher councils. On the other hand, a large part of the professors are determined to use every means to counter such developments; also the general public, disturbed by the ideological radicalism and the bad manners of some of the student activists, is inclined to give its vote to representatives who are dedicated to the restoration of 'law and order'.

It is interesting to note that, quite independently of the specific social and political system predominant in a given state, governments are in increasing measure inclined to react sternly against the rebellious students. In fact, some of them seem to welcome the occasion of curtailing or annulling the traditional autonomy of the universities. Most governments act in this respect as if they accepted Durkheim's interpretation of the prevailing situation as 'anomie', as a situation in which cultural, religious and all other non-political realms have ceased to function as sources of meaningful order and have handed over all order-creating power to the state. The student revolt, with all its flagrant attempts at the politicisation of consciousness and, through it, at the politicisation of all aspects of life, is nevertheless primarily a 'cultural' revolution. In the field of aesthetic awareness it fights against the material interests of the existing economic and political systems; in the field of political consciousness it dreams not less intensely of a universal, 'cultural' freedom after the abolition of all existing power relations. Compared with the opportunism of the progressive technocrats, the rebellious students are old-fashioned humanists. They are, we repeat, the heirs to the natural rights and natural law philosophy of the second part of the eighteenth century.

If we ask what effect the 'new awareness' and the 'new consciousness' will have on society as a whole as former hippies or provos or student rebels take up jobs in the existing order, we can do little more than guess. Some will adjust to the routine which is asked of them and perhaps save some of the old spirit for leisure-time activities. Others may try to forget their former feelings, thoughts and experiences as expressions of a transitory, youthful stage in their life. Again others will try to maintain and enhance their new awareness and consciousness in their new 'adult' environment. As architects and city planners they will try to build more humane, more attractive housing units; as members of various civic boards and political organisations they will consider social problems as more than cases; as teachers they will respect the personality – the handicaps and promises – of each pupil; as engineers and scientists they will be aware of their own play instinct and the play instinct of others; as citizens they will not shrink from dirty, unpopular or hopeless tasks.

Uncertain as we are of the effect of the agitations of 'youth' on our society, we can be sure of two things: that the phenomenon of 'youth', typical of advanced industrial societies, will be with us as long as such societies exist; and that, whatever happens to 'youth' and its social, political and cultural attempts, the problems that agitate 'youth' will not abandon us.

BIBLIOGRAPHY

Corsini, Gianfranco, 'Berkeley on the Tiber', *Nation*, 10 June 1968.

Crick, Bernard, and Robson, William A. (eds), *Protest and Discontent* (Harmondsworth: Penguin Books, for *Political Quarterly*, 1970). Contains a number of excellent essays.

Deutsche Jugend. A monthly magazine published by the German Youth Institute, Munich. Contains much useful and up-to-date information.

Feuer, Lewis, *Conflict of Generations* (New York: Basic Books; London: Heinemann, 1969).

Fyvel, T. R., *The Insecure Offenders: Rebellious Youth in the Welfare State* (Harmondsworth: Penguin Books, 1969). Primarily on youth gangs.

Gretton, John, *Students and Workers* (London: Macdonald, 1969).

Institute for Social Research Monographs, University of Zagreb. In Serbo-Croat with English summaries; contains the results of empirical research on various aspects of youth in Yugoslavia.

Kennan, George, *Democracy and the Student Left* (London: Hutchinson, 1968).

Loewenthal, Richard, *Der romantische Rückfall* (Stuttgart: Kohlhammer, 1970).

Mannheim, Karl, *Essays on the Sociology of Knowledge* (New York: Oxford U.P., 1952).

Marcuse, Herbert, An Essay on Liberation (Boston: Beacon Press, 1969).

—— *et al.*, *Marx und die Revolution* (Frankfurt: Suhrkamp, 1970).

Neidhardt, Friedhelm, *et al.*, *Jugend im Spektrum der Wissenschaften* (Munich: Juventa, 1970). Contains a number of significant theoretical essays.

Robinson, Paul A., *The Freudian Left* (New York: Harper Colophon Books, 1969). A useful presentation of the ideas of Reich and Marcuse.

Roszak, Theodore, *The Making of a Counter-Culture* (New York, 1969). A sympathetic account of the aesthetic side of the American youth culture.

Schelsky, Helmut, *Die skeptische Generation* (Düsseldorf, 1956).

Spender, Stephen, *The Year of the Young Rebels* (London: Weidenfeld & Nicolson, 1969).

Straub, Sylvia, *Ursachen und Erscheinungsformen bei der Bildung jugendlicher Banden* (Winterthur, 1965). A systematic study of the origin and composition of youth gangs.

Vincent, Gérard, 'Les Lycéens et la Politique: Essai sur la perception de la politisation des lycéens à travers les sondages et enquêtes récents', s.l.e.a. (reprint). The results of empirical research done in two French state schools.

Wills, Garry, 'The Making of the Yippie Culture', *Esquire* (Nov 1969).

NOTES

1. Cf. Friedhelm Neidhardt, 'Bezugspunkte einer soziologischen Theorie der Jugend', in *Jugend im Spektrum der Wissenschaften* (Munich, 1970) p. 18.

2. Cf. T. R. Fyvel, *The Insecure Offenders: Rebellious Youth in the Welfare State* (Harmondsworth : Penguin Books, 1969); Marcel Hicter, 'Eine an der Jugend krankende Gesellschaft', *Deutsche Jugend*, no. 11 (Nov 1968); Sylvia Straub, *Ursachen und Erscheinungsformen bei der Bildung jugendlicher Banden* (Winterthur, 1965).

3. Dieter Baake, 'Untergrund : Einheit und Aspekte', *Merkur*, VI (1970).

4. Daniel Bell, 'Unstable America', *Encounter*, XXXIV (June 1970), pp. 11 ff.

5. Cf. Theodore Roszak, *The Making of a Counter-Culture* (New York, 1969).

6. Ibid., p. 175.

7. New York, 1954.

8. New York, 1962.

9. Cf. Garry Wills, 'The Making of the Yippie Culture', *Esquire* (Nov 1969) pp. 135 ff.

10. Ibid.

11. Cf. G. E. L. Boon von Ochsee, 'Das Phänomen der Provos', *Deutsche Jugend*, no. 2 (Feb 1968).

12. Jutta Kamke, 'Der Sozialismus der zärtlichen Hand', *Die Zeit*, no. 49 (4 Dec 1970) p. 68.

13. Helmut Schelsky, *Die skeptische Generation* (Düsseldorf, 1956).

14. Karl Mannheim, *Essays on the Sociology of Knowledge* (New York, 1952) pp. 304 ff.

15. Gianfranco Corsini, 'Berkeley on the Tiber', *Nation*, 10 June 1968.

16. Cf. Jirina Siklová, 'Jugend und Jugendsoziologie in der Tschechoslowakei', *Deutsche Jugend*, no. 6 (June 1968).

17. Cf. Manfred Riedel, *Wandel des Generationsproblems in der modernen Gesellschaft* (Düsseldorf and Köln, 1969) p. 34.

18. James Jupp, 'The Discontents of Youth', in *Protest and Discontent,* ed. Bernard Crick and William A. Robson (Harmondsworth : Penguin Books, for *Political Quarterly,* 1970) p. 75.

19. Werner Loch, 'Generationskonflikt und Demokratie', *Deutsche Jugend,* no. 5 (May 1968).

20. Richard Loewenthal, *Romantischer Rückfall* (Stuttgart, 1970) p. 10.

21. Ibid., p. 31.

22. Ibid., p. 8.

23. Ibid., p. 35.

24. *Süddeutsche Zeitung,* No. 121 (25 May 1970) p. 16.

25. Cf. E. P. Thompson, 'The Extra-Parliamentary Opposition', in Crick and Robson (eds), *Protest and Discontent.*

26. Herbert Marcuse, *An Essay on Liberation* (Boston : Beacon Press, 1969) p. 23.

27. Ibid.

28. Cf. Paul A. Robinson, *The Freudian Left* (New York : Harper Colophon Books, 1969) p. 5.

29. Ibid., p. 189.

30. Ibid., p. 240.

31. Ibid.

32. Ibid., p. 243.

33. Herbert Marcuse, 'Political Preface 1966', quoted by Robinson, *The Freudian Left,* p. 244.

34. Henry Cavanna, 'Protest in France', in Crick and Robson (eds), *Protest and Discontent,* p. 200.

35. Trevor Fisk, 'The Nature and Causes of Student Unrest', ibid., p. 82.

36. Peter Sedgwick, 'Varieties of Socialist Thought', ibid., p. 55.

37. Cavanna, ibid., p. 195.

38. Ibid., p. 197.

39. Cf. Carlo Donolo, *Kurbuch 13* (Frankfurt am Main, 1968).

40. A. H. Hanson, 'Some Literature on Student Revolt', Crick and Robson (eds), *Protest and Discontent,* pp. 142–3.

41. Gérard Vincent, 'Les Lycéens et la Politique : Essai sur la perception de la politisation des lycéens à travers les sondages et enquêtes récents' s.l.e.a. (reprint).

INDEX